LAKE GARDA

Published by KINA ITALIA

LAKE GARDA

© Editions KINA ITALIA S.p.A. - Milan
Realization and printing by KINA Italia S.p.A. - Milan
Exclusive sales agent: Poiatti Pietro - Nave (BS)
text by Attilio Mazza
Pagination by Mr. Renzo Matino

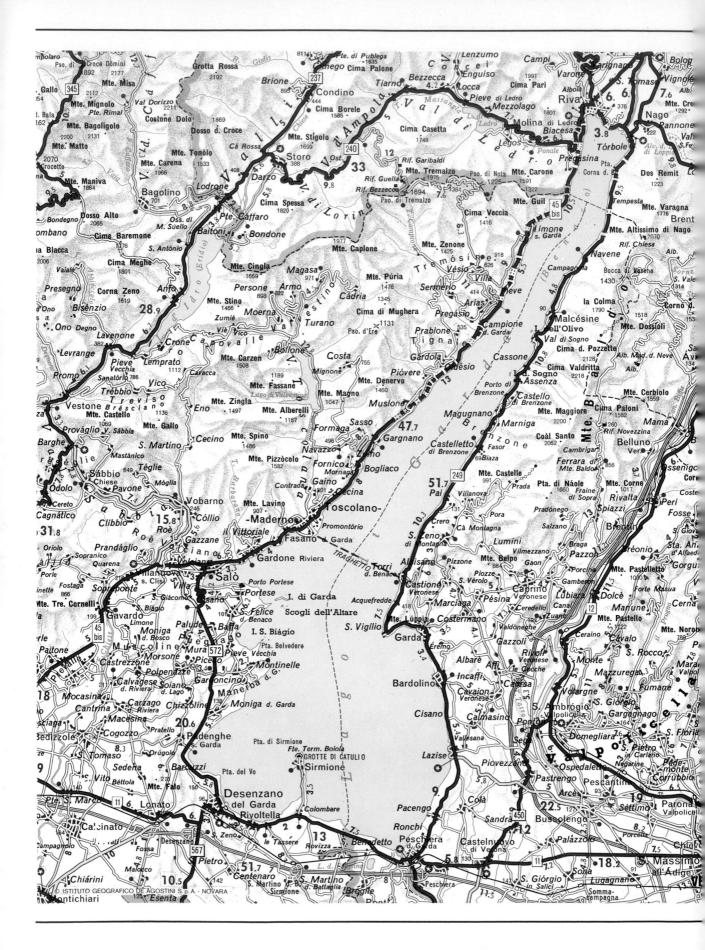

LAKE GARDA

Lake Garda is an island of incomparable scenery, a mediterranean spot immersed in the savage grandeur of the alpine mountains. It is a combination of remote historic events and of human history. Nature and history come together said Carlo Cattaneo, describing in 1844 this corner of paradise: "An even greater marvel awaits the traveller if descending from the summit of Baldo, where he had been gathering Bavarian sandstone, the pallene spinosa, purple cytisus, he could see the flaming bunches of oleander already through the cracks in the rocks of Limone. Further in the on laughing amphitheatre of Bogliaco he would even see, as if among the immense colonnades of Persèpoli or Menfi, the bizzare constructions of the citrus plants. He would see the delicate Capparis flower nestling between the breakers on the shore of Salodiano and a continuous forest of bay trees, dotted with the odd cedar and orange tree, their bright foliage alternating with the austere tints of the grey olive-groves, strewing balmy gold under a limpid sky".

A place where man's interference has been respectful of nature, the environmental beauty reaches levels difficult to surpass; like the "green Sirmio" which "smiles in the clear lake, flower of the peninsulas".

Geography

Lake Garda is situated 65 metres above sea level; it has a length, from Riva to Peschiera, of 51.6 km; it has a maximum width of 17.2 km; a perimeter of 155 km; a surface area of 389.98 km^2: the maximum depth (between Muslone and Castelletto di Brenzone) is 346 m; the average depth is 135 m.

The principal tributary is the Sarca which exiting near Peschiera takes the name Minchio. An artificial drainage system, to the north of the lake, near Torbole, directs the water from the Adige into Garda during the periods of high water level. The waters of the lake are also added to by numerous torrents, as well as by underground springs. Among these it is worth pointing out the Bojola Spring which comes out of the ground near Sirmione. This is virgin water with volcanic origins, which gushes out of the living rock at the bottom of the lake, at a depth of 19 m, at a temperature of 69.9 °C. This water has healing powers noted since 1500.

Lake Garda is bordered to the east by Mount Baldo which separates it from the valley of the Adige; to the west by a chain of steep mountains, making it look like a fjord, with impressive bays opening into it. To the south it is bordered by a line of morainic hills which run from Salò up to the foot slopes of Mount Baldo.

Picturesque roads run along all banks of the lake (those on the western side of Garda are particularly attractive) while others branch off inland, offering tourists the chance to reach enchanting places.

200 metres from the headland of S. Felice, at Valtenesi, is the Isle of Garda, the largest and most important among those which dot the lake's shores. It is 110 metres long and has an average width of 65 metres.

There are several winds common to Garda, such as the *Sover* or *Suer* (called *Balì* on the bank of Trento) which blows from Bocca di Riva and disappears towards S. Vigilio. The *Ander* is often violent. It blows from wrest to east and brings good weather when it begins after midday and stops before sunset, bad weather when it blows during the morning, in which case it predicts a change in the weather. The *Avreser* (Balestro) blows from every direction and brings scattered clouds and changeable weather. The evening winds are called *Montesè*, which means mountainous. From the west comes the *Ora* which is a regular wind and helps navigation. The *Rèfol* is a spring wind, sudden and short (from *el moresa*, meaning flirts). In the winter, the *Gardesana* or *Grancher* or *Luganot* arrives from the gableboard; it brings fog or variable weather. From the mouth of Vorbano (above Salò) comes the *Bovaren* which brings cold weather. Administratively Garda belongs to three regions (Lombardy, Veneto and Trentino) and to three provinces (Brescia, Verona and Trento). The villages of the lake are grouped into one community (Community of Garda).

The Origins

Antonio Stoppani, writing about the origins of Garda, put forward a fascinating hypothesis: a marine fjord reemerging in the Pliocene period. More modern scientists however seem to be agreed on the "benacense syncline" (the concave extension taking place in the Miocene period) and on excavations by glaciers in the Quarternery period. In the Neogene period the "benacense fate" was established: the impressive contrast between the Brescian and Veronese banks; the design of the picturesque rocks, with their ruinous-looking precipices. However Garda, up until the end of the Pliocene period, apart from some aspects, which had already formed, did not yet exist in its present form. It took four Quaternary glaciations, which with repeatedly excavating action, scoured out a much longer basin to remove the crumbly rocks of the "benacense syncline". The glaciers, with varying advances and withdrawals, gave form to the morainic hills which enclose the Gardesian basin to the south, towards the plain, with what looks like a festoon of multiple hoops.

This fascinating chapter on the geological history of Garda is still being enlarged by scholars in order to understand it's full importance. The hypothesis of a fifth glaciation—Donau—reemerging over seven-hundred thousand years ago has also been put forward. In this temporal dimension it is not easy to understand the reason for great changes, the variations of climate which between one glaciation and another determined the development of vegetation and afterwards the multiplication of fauna and thus its habitability for man.

The Flora

Through the millenniums of geological history to today. The benacense (area around lake Garda) landscape was determined by a series of factors: the position at only 65 metres above sea level; the moderating action of the water (389 km^2 of surface with a volume of almost 50 km^3) on the temperature of the air; the barriers of mountains that protect it from the north winds; the relatively modest amount of water brought in by the tributaries and thus the limitation of the cooling effect on the mass of water (recently however controversy has arisen as to the possibilities of grave ecobiological mutations due to the dumping through the artificial canal at Torbole); the low rainfall (between one thousand and one thousand two hundred millimetres a year) with concentrated precipitation, mostly in the spring or in the autumn; stable thermic values (mild summer temperature and high winter one). For these reasons many characteristics of the climate of Garda resemble the submediterranean ones of the Ligurian Riviera. The mild winter temperature permits the flowering of numerous periwinkles, heather, daises, and small geraniums. The spring comes early: in March the mild weather is already inducing to outdoor life. The summer is long, dry and sunny. The autumn is short, with typical autumn showers. It is therefore noticeable that the general mediterranean character, acquires particular value according to the natural position of each part of the lake (the inlets, sheltered from the winds, on the southern shores; the hot, rocky slopes to the north) thus favouring a remarkable variety of vegetation.

The Fauna

The terrestrial fauna of Garda was almost completely destroyed with the disappearence of the last age-old forests. Once many areas (The Valtenese, Mount Baldo, the mountainous inland area of the western bank) were the home of deer, roe deer, wolves and wild boars; not to mention the flying species which, from the water to the summits of the morainic hills to the south and the high areas along the two main banks, were the joy of naturalists.

A small, but interesting sample of winged species from the Gardesan area can still be admired in the collection preserved by the ancient abbey of Maguzzano di Lonato. The ignorance of man now seems to be completing its destructive cycle, increasing mortality among the more rare species of fish and creating alterations in the equilibrium of the water. This is happening to the Garda carp (*Salmo carpio*): only prompt action based on precise ecological knowledge could now ensure it's survival.

History

The mild climate, the beauty of the countryside, the richness of nature—luxuriant woods, populated by a rich and copious fauna—all encouraged the first human settlements. The earliest traces of the presence of man are carved on the rocks of Mount Baldo (a recent discovery). Who these first inhabitants were is not known. On the other hand the lives of other ancient inhabitants can be more clearly traced. According to the historian Antonio Fappani, they left clear traces in the prehistoric settlements of Polada and in the peat bogs of Polpenazze (where even a prehistoric piroga was found) as well as the settlements found at Desenzano, Bor, Pacengo, Bardolino, Cisano etc. The Ligurians and the Euganians were accompanied by or followed by, the Etruscans, the Enetites, the Eisacks, the Erectus and the Celts. Then it was the turn of the Cenomanes who took over from the native population.

This continous alternation of the ancient inhabitants can be reconstructed using the toponymys and grave-stones, like the relatively famous one of Voltino with its bilingual inscription. The very name Benaco, according to some scholars of Celtic origins, derives from *benncorno*, peninsula peak and must therefore mean "lake of the peninsulas".

The Romans in 152 B.C. drove out or subjugated the Cenomanes; in 89 B.C. they granted the Latin law to the Transpadians and fourty years later Roman citizenship. The western bank of the Riviera, up to the northern limits (including the territory of Arco) was ascribed to the Fabia tribe; the eastern bank (together with Verona) passed to the Polibia tribe. The Garda basin, from then on, was almost always divided into two or three administrative departments. The testimony to the Romans on Garda is impressive: from Sirmione to Desenzano and to Salò; from Toscolano to Riva, monuments, both large and small, document an era of intense and splendid life on Garda. Not even the barbaric invasions (Ostrogothic, Heruli Gothic, Alemannian) succeded in eliminating them; neither did the successive Byzantine and Longobard dominations (the latter was very important).

In this era, Christianity was first known to have been spread by some Bishop saints (St. Vigil, St. Euprerio, and especially St. Ercolano). Thus the first Christian communities sprang up at Tremosine, Castelletto di Brenzone and Sirmione, as the most ancient churches show.

The Carolingian domination, following the Longobardian one, had to surrender to the barbaric invasions in defense of which, in the IXth century A.D., the fortified enclosures were built (some of which are still visible today) in Padenghe, Moniga, Maderno, Lonato etc. In 899 the Huns destroyed the monastery at Maguzzano which was rebuilt centuries later. The rock of Garda became the refuge of Adelaide, the widow of Lotario and later the wife of Ottone. The different emperors conceded numerous fiefs on Garda, while Maderno, Manerba, Salò, and Desenzano took on particular importance in the infinite disputes between the various factions and the army forces.

In the XIIIth century the Patarine heresy was particularly powerful on Garda (especially at Sirmione): it's leader Brother Dolcine ended up on the stake along with 170 followers on the 13th February 1278 at Verona.

The period of municipal autonomy was particularly vivacious, with strange rules and statutes. It was also open ground to the battles between the Guelfa and Ghibellina factions, between the signori of Ezzelino da Romano and the Scaligeri and the Visconti di Pandolfo Malatesta. In the XIth century the traditional division on Garda between Brescia and Verona was established and the power of the Bishop-Prince of Trento who obtained the right of navigation on the 9th of February 1182, from the Emporer Frederick I. Ten years later on 26th-27th July 1192, the Emporer Henry VI gave Brescia jurisdiction over all the territory on the central-western bank, from Pozzolengo to Limone. To free itself from the rule of the Scaligeri and the Visconti, the Community of Garda came into being in the first half of the XIVth century, as a confederation of the Brescian communities on Garda. After resisting an attempted takeover by Cangrande and by Mastino della Scala, signori from Verona, the community consolidated it's statutes in 1334 by placing itself under the protection of Venice and appointed itself a Magnifica Patria. The protectorate of Venice over the Riviera was relatively short: it lasted from 1339 to 1351. Then followed the hard-fought dominion of the Visconti di Milano which, far from ending the autonomy of the Magnifica Patria, recognised in 1419 by the same Filippo Maria Visconti, actually consolidated it. This autonomy—which was never independence—was reconfirmed by the Republic of Venice, when the Riviera made an act of dedication to it on 13th May 1426. In payment for the loyalty shown during the war against the army of Niccolò Piccinino, the Riviera became considered, by the Serenissima Republic of Venice, as separate land together with Valcamonica, Asola, Lonato etc. The Magnifica Patria defended its autonomy even against the demands of Brescia. However it obtained only the symbolic right of nominating a mayor, a right which gave rise to the difficult situation which led Venice to install a Venetian patrician with the title of "Captain of the Riviera and Supervisor of Salò" beside the mayor. The Magnifica Patria kept these rules up to 1797, tying its destiny irrevocably to Venice's, constituting a unique fact in the history of the Riviera, which was not repeated either on the Veronese or the Trentine banks.

On the Veronese bank, in the XIth century, an administrative district was set up, taking in the coastal communities from Malcesine to Lugana, elected as a county in 1131, with real autonomy and its own territorial council. In 1193 the dominion of Verona spread along the lake: the commune of this city acquired the Fortress of Garda from Henry VI and extended it's juridiction as far as the community of Sirmione. The Veronese territory then passed under the rule of Ezzelino da Romano, then under that of the Scaligeri and finally, in 1405, under that of Venice.

The chain of events at the extreme north of Garda was different: in the Longobard and Carolingian eras a Judicaria Summa Laganensis was set up (the Valli Giudicarie gets its name from it), whereby the authority of the Bishop of Trento, which became increasingly important, was added to that of the Benedictine monasteries of Leno, Brescia, Bobbio, Nonontola etc. It took the place of the Marca di Verona and in 976 passed on to the Duke of Carinzia to then be returned, with the decree of Henry II on the 9th April 1004, to the Bishop of Trento, raised to the position of Prince.

The donation was confirmed by Corrado II with a

decree on 31 May 1027. The bishop principality of Trento was thus made completely independent of any other jurisdiction.

This dominion defended itself against the repeated attempts by the counts of Tirolo and by the Hapsburgs to take control, until the annexation by the Austrians on 4th February 1803 .

In 1918 the population freed itself from this dominion to join Italy.

The facts relative to the governing of the water are different to those for the land. The Venetian Republic, assumed exclusive rights to it after Charles IV, in 1351, conceded to Mastino II della Scala, all the waters of the lake, with rights of navigation and fishing, rights which were passed on to the Viscontis, the Carraras, to the Scaligeris and thus to the Serene State of Venice in 1406. From 1426 to 1455 these rights on the waters were administrated by the Supervisor and Captain of Salò and afterwards by the Captain of Malcesine. The Trentine authorities, in the middle of the 17th century, contested these rights; however only in the 18th century was the dominion of the Hapsburgs set up on the southern part of the lake.

The fall of the Venetian dominion was caused by the Napoleonic armies in 1797. Opposed to him and the army of the Brescian Republic were the Valsabbines who had come down towards the lake. Military action between the Austrians and the French took place between 1801 and 1805; however, despite the differences, the Riviera passed to Austria in 1815. Many patriots raised their voices against the Austrian rule while between 1848 an 1868, the names of Pastrego, Peschiera, S. Martino, Solferino, and Custoza became famous due to their courage and Italian blood.

The history of the last hundred years is well--known: in 1848 Peschiera, which was part of the historic Quadrilateral (with Verona, Mantova and Legnago), fell into Italian hands. On the 24th June 1859 in the hills of S. Martino and Solferino the bloody battle which liberated Lombardy from Austrian rule was fought. In 1866 the Austrian gunboats bombarded Gargnano and the Brescian bank at exactly the same time as Garibaldi's volunteers were climbing from Val di Ledro towards Ponale. At Custoza they fought a tough and unfortunate battle which nevertheles won the whole Veronese bank for Italy. The high regions of Garda were the scene of fighting between 1915 and 1918, until the Italian offensive liberated all the territories, the last act of unification.

NAVIGATION ON GARDA

The remains of prehistoric pirogas confirm that man has always navigated on the waters of Lake Garda. Not until 1827, however, under the Austrian government, was a regular navigational service inaugurated, using the steamboat "Arciduca Ranieri" weighing 40 tons, with wharfs at Riva and at Desenzano. After the second war of independence the lake was divided into two: the northern half went to Austria the southern to Italy. The Society of Northern Italian Railways substituted the old gunboat anchored at Sirmione (the service was every fifteen days from Salò to Sirmione) with four steamboats. Only in 1888, with the Rete Adriatica Society, did two new steamboats enter into service. The service was strengthened and restructured in 1918 when all the Gardanese coasts finally passed over to Italy. The present navigation service is under the management of the government with regular trips the whole year round and tourist cruises in the summer period.

SIRMIONE

The Scaligeri castle or Fortress was built as a stronghold by Mastino della Scala, within the confines of the ancient walls surrounding the whole Medieval hamlet. For shape, structure and condition of conservation it is considered the finest of the surviving castles of the Scaligeri period. On the ground floor you can see architectural fragments and sculptures of different periods: from the keep (146 steps) you enjoy a wonderful

view of the town. From the inside staircases of the keep you can reach the patrol communication trenches. The peninsula of Sirmione leaning from south over the blue waters of Benaco for about 4 km, is much frequented for the splendour of its landscape and for its thermal treatments. The poets Catullo and Carducci, charmed by the beauty of these places, described them in immortal lines. The whole island (which joins the isthmus by a bridge, changing it into a peninsula) is like a wide, wonderful natural park, strewn with alleys and paths among a luxuriant vegetation of olive trees, cypresses, laurels and magnolias. Three hills rise inside, the first, eastward, is called "Cortine" the second, westward is "Malvino", the third northward, between the two, is called "Catullus's Caves" seat of the archaeological zone of an ancient Roman palace.

HISTORY. According to some scholars the peninsula probably derives its name from the ancient Greek word "syrma" (tail, train) or from the Gallic words "sirm" and "ona" (aquatic hotel). The peninsula was certainly inhabited from the remotest ages. The important Roman buildings, the tombstones, the trunks of the columns, the capitals and other relics found during the centuries testify the ancient importance of Sirmione,

which is mentioned as a town in Antonino's itinerary. The history of Sirmione does not stop at the Roman period. It was chosen by Queen Ansa, wife of Desiderio, King of the Longobards, to build a monastery of the Benedictines in the VIIIth cent. In the XIIth cent. Sirmione passed under the rule of the Scaligeri who built the fortress "the second among the castles of Europe for purity of form and ingeniousness of conception". The castle, conceived as a fortification, surrounded all the hamlet with its walls. The Visconti succeeded the Scaligeri, later the Carraresi of Padua. At the beginning of the XVth cent. Sirmione passed under Venice, following its vicissitudes.
TO SEE. The Scaligero Castle. Catullus's Caves. Great St. Mary's parish church. The small church of St. Peter in Mavino.

Great St. Mary's Church of the XV century has a columned portico outiside. One of these columns belongs to the ruins of an ancient Roman temple. Under the portico there are tomb inscriptions of the XVIIIth century. Of interest inside are: The statue of the Virgin, the XVIIIth century pulpit and organ in finely carved wood with friezes and inlays; votive frescos by artists of the first half of the XVIth century, paintings on canvas representing St. Andrew and St. Jerome by Voltolini and a Crucifix considered the work of F. Brusasorzi.

SIRMIONE. Great St Mary's Church (XV cent.).

SIRMIONE. Great St Mary's Church (XV-XVI cent. frescos).

Archaeological Walk. It starts from the *panoramic road* which leads to the lake, with delightful views of the scenery on the background of the waters. In the small patch of open ground from where one descends to the lake, there are famous and important ruins known as the *Great Pillar* and the *Great Archways* (four). On the right side (facing the archways) there is a short stairway leading to a large room with a barrel vault (with four niches where the discoveries from the latest digs are assembled) called the *Horse Grotto* because some relics of a horse were unearthed here: in 1500 it was probably used as a stable. Climbing another stairway and turning immediately left we come to the *Long Corridor* on whose background there is the *Three-mullioned Window of Paradise*. Along this "corridor" we see on the left the *Giants Room* (so called because of the big stones found here), the largest room in the villa.

The Double Cryptoporticus is the sector of greatest architectural interest. According to Dr. Mirabella Roberti — on whose "guidance" we have relied for these notes — the long "arcade, now without a roof, extended from one end of the construction, from N to S for 159 m and was composed of two corridors each 4.20 m wide, separated by a line of 64 pillars forming an arcade which supported two large barrel vaults (fragments can be seen here and there) in concrete with pieces of porous tufa". It was also used for taking a stroll on sultry days. Situated on the outside are the so-called Botteghe (shops) claimed, by those who disagree with Dr. Mirabella Roberti, to be the commercial area of the spa or possibly ruins of the Longobard monastery of Queen Ansa.

The swimming pool. In a large rectangular room (18.30 m by 8.10) there are four flights of steps leading down to a vast pool. The large rectangular room was built later; it was heated by means of warm air which passed beneath the brick floor. It was the "tepidarium" of the villa's private spa; close to it there were rooms for sweating ("sudationes") and for the cold bath ("frigidarium").

The "Antiquarium". The most precious relics are collected here, including oillamps, pieces of vases, fibulas, fragments of plasters, of decorative stuccoes, of frescoes (with fruit and birds, sacrifice scenes, female figures, etc.). The photographical report of the complex of monuments and of the excavations is also interesting.

Church of St. Peter in Mavino. A very old church in Romanesque style. It was first built in the VIIIth century, in the following centuries (XI-XIV cent.) it underwent several modifications. It sits on the top of Mavino hill, on the ruins of an ancient pagan temple. Inside, on the walls and in the apses there are valuable frescoes of the XV and XVI cent.

St. Anne's Church at the Fortress.

This is probably the church that strikes the tourists more. It is situated right at the entrance to the inhabited area just after the drawbridge on the left, adjoining the castle walls. The church — dedicated to St. Anne, the Virgin's mother — was built around 1400 specially to offer a religious service to the garrison of the castle and to the inhabitants of the surrounding area. It now belongs to the town council and it is almost always open to the public, including at night. With its candles lighting up the votive image, it confers an evocative atmosphere to this wonderful area in Sirmione. Some people claim it was first erected in the late fourteenth century, while the cross vault was built in the fifteenth century and the barrel vault is supposed to date back to the seventeenth century. The church has a single aisle and only one altar; the small presbytery, built in the eighteenth century, is decorated with stuccos which break the harmony of the whole. The votive frescos painted by varius artists - date back to the early sixteenth century. The Virgin on the altar is painted on stone with the Scaligeri's coat of arms.

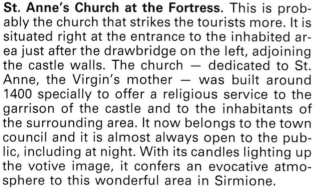

Frescos (XV-XVI cent.).

SOLFERINO

Like S. Martino, it belongs to the historical events of Italy because of the battle on June 24, 1859 between the Franco-Piedmontese and the Austrian army. The war memorial is in the Church of St. Peter. Of remarkable importance is the Fortress, a powerful tower of 1022, restored in 1661 and turned into a military museum in memory of the bloody battle. In Solferino, the Swiss philanthropist Henry Dunant winner of the Nobel peace prize, struck by the suffering and the great number of wounded soldiers, founded the famous humanitarian institution known as the "International Red Cross". In 1959 the Memorial was erected on the Hill of the Cypresses which all the nations adhering to the Convention of Geneva contributed to.

S. MARTINO DELLA BATTAGLIA.
The Tower.

ABBAZIA DI MAGUZZANO

The old Benedictine "Abbey" of Maguzzano was built beside a Roman road at the end of the VIII century. It was burnt by the Huns around 922 and devastated by Visconti's troops in 1438. Attached to the Congregation of St. Giustina of Padua for Verona (Poor Servants of Divine Providence). The Abbey contains a fine collection of stuffed birds of which there are 1000 specimens.

The Abbey is at present a place of prayer. Throughout the year it organizes and offers hos-

thirty years, in 1491 it was entrusted to the Monastery of St Benedict Po. Almost entirely rebuilt from its foundations, it was embellished by the beautiful Renaissance church and by the *elegant cloister* which presents such pure and harmonious architectural lines as to be considered one of the finest works the history of Brescian art can boast.

The illustrious Cardinal Reginaldo Polo (1500-1558) was a guest here in 1533. From here, he carried out an intense diplomatic activity (about 50 documents) to prepare England's return to the Church.

Suppressed by Napoleon in 1797, the Abbey passed into private ownership and in 1904-38 was inhabited by Cistercian Trappist monks. It is now the property of the Opera Don Calabria di

pitality for: spiritual exercises, retreats for groups and individuals, study days, gatherings, prayer meetings. It has ample space for movement indoors, in the cloister, and in the Abbey grounds.

The severity of the surroundings, the silence, the picturesque garden, the view and the climate of the lake, make this Abbey a wonderful place for one who seeks an oasis of peace and spirituality.

The Abbey of Maguzzano (Lonato).

DESENZANO DEL GARDA

This picturesque small town, situated on the south part of the lake in the large gulf of the same name, has a large port, the widest and best equipped of Garda, and an old, characteristic, small port surrounded by old buildings on three sides. Desenzano is the headquaters of the Navigation Company on the whole lake. One of the most important centres, it has recently undergone large commercial, tourist and residential development.

HISTORY. Desenzano was one of the first places on Garda to be inhabited by man in prehistoric times after the withdrawal of glaciers; the ruins of the Polada civilisation, discovered in 1873, on the way to Lonato, prove it.

The prehistoric site discovered during excavations of peat is still shrouded in mystery, in spite of the numerous objects, tools and fossil remains come to light and kept at the Ethnographic Museum in Rome. The Roman period was particularly flourishing; it was the scene of a victory over the Goths (269). There is a lot evidence of that period including the remains of a villa, which are particularly important.

It was invaded by the Barbarians and given by Charlemagne to the monks of St. Zeno in 879. It was a fief of Count Ugone and in 1426 came under the Republic of Venice. After the fall of Venice it was joined to Brescia whose destiny it followed. The Venetian period had a great influence on the development of the town; in that period the weekly market became famous (which still now is held on Tuesdays); it was an opportunity for all the regions to exchange produce with Venice.

We must remember the high speed flying school founded at Desenzano from 1927 to 1936 where Agello and De Bernardi, piloting seaplanes, conquered many speed records; a monument was dedicated to these pioneers in 1967.

Among the famous personalities of Desenzano we remember Angela Merici (1470-1540), sanctified in 1807. She dedicated her life to girls' education, founding the congregation of the Angeline. Giosué Carducci stayed at Desenzano, serving periodically on the Royal Lyceum Committee. Signs of this period can be seen in his poetical works.

TO SEE. The Roman villa of the IIIrd cent. B.C. St. Mary Magdalene parish church.

CHARACTERISTIC POINTS. The old port, surrounded on three sides by buildings, among which is the town hall and that of the supervisor, which is Venetian, both designed by Todeschini; the lakeside promenade.

The small characteristic port.

◀ *The port.* *Panorama.*

◀ *The lakeside and port at night.*

The Roman Villa. This grand construction or at least the most important part, was discovered relatively recently, that is at the end of 1921, in the area of Borgo Regio, now called Roman Excavations Road. The name is quite important: Borgo Regio, it is presumed, could have been the original site of the city. If this hypothesis is true, Desenzano would have arisen around an agricultural nucleus, concentrated around a villa. The

Polychrome pavement mosaics (III cent. B.C.).

most important part left to us of the whole complex is the reception area of the villa, with an almost square courtyard in the middle, surrounded, at one time, by a portico with six columns on each side except to the north. To the west is the house's main reception room, the oecus, where particularly interesting mosaics have been found, such as the one commonly called "Running Animals". The floor mosaics are the most unusual and interesting aspect of this monument: the colours are extremely vivid; there are many illustrated scenes, set in relief in rich framings. Other mosaics have rich geometric elaborations; they are all unforgettable for their joyous palette. Long neglection has caused severe damage, howerver the present arrangement and patronage allow for an interesting visit.

St. Mary Magdalene Church goes back to 1480. It was rebuilt in 1586 according to G. Todeschini's project. The temple facade is in Doric with an XVIII century Baroque door. Inside, there are the very interesting Doric columns and the XV century wooden statue of Mary Magdalen, the XVIII century high altar to the Redeemer with little statues, inlays and rich decorations in polychrome marble, valuable paintings by Zenon Veronese, D. Cignaroli of the XVIII century, by D. Riccio of the XVI century, by A. Celesti, a Venetian painter of the XVII century and works in tempera by G. Anselmi. In the Blessed Sacrement chapel there are four Corinthian columns and the valuable altar-piece "the Last Supper" by G.B. Tiepolo.

G.B. Tiepolo - "The Last Supper" Detail.

MANERBA

HISTORY. The ancient Minervae Arx is today an important tourist centre which has developed mainly in recent years. There were settlements there even before the Roman era. However, the history of Manerba is closely tied to its fortress (of which, unfortunately, today nothing remains): it was the site, in 776, of the final resistance of the Longobards commanded by Cacone (nephew of King Desiderio), against Charlemagne. The fortress passed to Beniamino da Manerba and then to the Scaligera family, the Viscontis, and the Venetians until in 1787, having become the haunt of a band of criminals, it was razed to the ground by order of the Superintendent of Salò. Innumerable stories and legends have grown up around the fortress, the best known of which are those collected in the book "The Brescian Valvassors" by the Brescian writer Lorenzo Ercolani.

Great importance is attached to the Pieve or Parish Church which goes back to the XI century, from which descended all the chapels of the Valtenesi area, later raised to parish churches with the exception of that of Padenghe. The Pieve of St Mary, with the Roman vicus, is the earliest evidence of Valtenesi unity.

TO SEE. The precipice on which the fortress stood (known as the "Manerba Fortress" and similar, according to some, depending on the point from which it is viewed, to Dante's profile); in the village of Solarolo the XVII century parish church and the ancient Church of St. John which belonged to the Knights of Jerusalem; in the village of Pieve Vecchia, the Church of St Mary of the Marches one of the oldest on the riviera of Lake Garda and the most precious monument in the entire area.

MANERBA. The magnificent, wide gulf.

VALTENESI

Dotted about with castles, noted for its vineyards, the Valtenesi area lies between Desenzano and the Gulf of Salò in a vast region of morainic hills. The Valtenesi area can be divided into the low, or coastal part, formed by the Communes of Padenghe, Moniga, Manerba, San Felice and the upper, or hilly, part, represented by the small centres of Puegnago, Polpenazze and Soiano. The Valtenesi riviera stretches along some twenty kilometres of lakeside characterized by picturesque creeks and promontories still not fully exploited from a tourist point of view, but which offer delightful and unusual views of extensive olive groves punctuated with vineyards. This part of the Valtenesi includes around thirty parks equipped for camping and tourist villages: a true paradise for lovers of the open air life. The upper Valtenesi centres, built high on rocky promontories from which wide vistas of the lake can be seen, themselves add greatly to the interest of the landscapes. Residential tourism has recently spread to these small centres, which are connected by a good panoramic road through the foothills, which winds from Padenghe to Puegnago. They still retain their agricultural character and undoubtedly represent places of considerable interest for an excursion. All the Valtenesi centres both in the upper and low regions are famous for their wine production: the local wines "Chiaretto" and "Groppello" can be bought at farms and wine cellars.

THE ISLE OF GARDA

From a geographical point of view, the Isle of Garda, one kilometre long and 60 metres wide, belongs to Valtenesi. It is the largest and finest island of the lake, with luxuriant parks and a beautiful private Venetian villa.

HISTORY. The Isle of Garda has had different names, derived from the families who owned it: Lechi, Ferrari, Borghese. It is known also as the Isle of the Friars: in 1200 Benjamin of Manerba gave it to St. Francis of Assisi who built a convent there. However these were not the first monks to inhabit it. In 879 Charlemagne had given it to the friars of St. Zeno. On this island, in 1421, St. Bernardino of Siena did penance. 400 years later the Marquis Luigi Lechi, who became its proprietor, built a great palace on the perimeter of the convent where he gave hospitality to the men of letters of that period. In 1820 the island was a centre of Carbonaro plots; this is the reason why Lechi was arrested and tried in Venice with Pellico, Confalonieri and other patriots. In 1860 the island passed under the Italian State which fortified it. But later it came under private ownership again. The Scipiones Borghese rebuilt the palace in Venetian style, giving it its present appearance.

The Isle of Garda.

POLPENAZZE

HISTORY. In the area of the ancient lake Lucone (dried up in 1458) researchers from the Gavardo Caves Group have found signs of one of the most ancient settlements in the Gardesan area. In the course of excavations from 1965 to 1969 prehistoric relics were unearthed which date from the Bronze Age (second millenium B.C.). Of particular interest are: a wooden piroga, numerous ceramic vases, objects made of bones and stone, all kept in the museum at Gavardo. On the shores of Lake Lucone there grew, in past centuries, scordium, a well known salutary herb. Polpenazze is nowadays a famous and important wine-producing centre. A wine fair is held every year in May.

TO SEE. The most ancient part of the town, near the town hall, which conserves medieval features; the church square from which an evocative view of Valtenesi and the lake can be enjoyed.

THE GAVARDO CAVES GROUP CIVIC MUSEUM. Piroga and prehistoric vases of the bronze age.

POLPENAZZE. Panorama.

PUEGNAGO

HISTORY. An agricultural village of Roman origin as proved by the name *Privinianum*, few signs remain of its ancient origins. Only a tombstone at the east door of the parish church is evidence that the Roman Goddess of Victory was worshipped here. The parish church depended from the old Pieve of St. Mary of Manerba. Its connection with the other villages of the Valtenesi is also shown by its membership of the *quadra* during the Venetian domination.

TO SEE. The three small lakes of Sovenigo, in which pile dwelling settlements have been found. Fabulous views can be enjoyed from the whole area.

SOIANO

HISTORY. According to some the name means *Solis ianua*, gate to the sun (and the smiling village really is caressed by the first rays of the sun); according to others it derives from *soi*, in dialect-gerda a small tub, and in fact there is one in the centre of the village coat of arms. It is known that this place was inhabited in prehistoric times, then by the Romans and by other peoples. Here too a castle was built in defence of barbarian invasions (it is still well preserved). Soiano had its own statutes in the time of the communes, while during the Venetian domination it was joined to the Valtenesi *quadra*.

TO SEE. The castle (a splendid panorama is visible from one of the towers; the XVII century Parish Church of St. Michael with its XVII century organ made by Franchino da Montechiaro; the peat bog behind the cemetery where prehistoric remains have been found.

Panorama.

S. FELICE DEL BENACO

The Sanctuary of Our Lady of Carmine of the XV century. The building in medieval style, has a Romanesque-Gothic architecture, with an ogival door and a plain central rose window. The build-ing goes back to the XV century. The basilica-shaped interior has a single nave with bare beams, divided by four ogive arches. The frescoes are interesting for the variety of subjects

and styles of the XV, XVI, XVII cent. There are clear influences of Mantegna, Foppa and Perugino. There are remarkable paintings: a Madonna on the throne with the Infant of the XV century, a medieval style crucifixion in green clay, four Saints ascribed to the Perugino school and the Annunciation, a valuable work of the XV century.
HISTORY. An important centre in Roman times, S. Felice still has the characteristics of an agricultural district. Numerous signs of the Roman era remain, particularly tombstones, one of which, dedicated to Neptune is embedded into the east side of the bell-tower of the parish church. The castle (of which only a few ruins remain) may have been built on the ruins of a Roman fort. Manara's volunteers who attempted to conquer the fortress of Peschiera, took refuge in it in 1848.
TO SEE. The XVI century parish church dedicated to Saints Felix and Adauto, built on the remains of a pagan temple, has some paintings of interest, including one attributed to the school of Tiepolo; the Carmine Sanctuary, an interesting XV century construction which, from 1452, belonged to the Carmelo di Mantova monks, was suppressed by Napoleon, restored and reopened for worship in 1952 by the same order. There are some interesting XV and XVI century frescoes to be admired there. Portese, a large and much visited village at one end of the Gulf of Salò, in an enchanting position and with a characteristic port; the *Baia del Vento* (Windy Bay), a picturesque inlet ending with St. Fermo's Cape (on which stands a fifteenth century church, the only remaining evidence of the older castle), extreme point of the S. Felice promontory at 220 metres from the Island of Garda.

SALÒ

Salò is one of the most important commercial and tourist centres of the West Riviera of Garda. It lies in a wide, pleasant gulf on the slopes of St. Bartholomew's Mount. From the neighbouring hills, adorned with villas and olive yards, you can admire the grandiosity and beauty of the lake.

HISTORY. According to a legend, Salò was founded by Queen Salonina or by the lucomone Saloo. There is little evidence of the Roman Slodium, only some tombstones kept in the town hall.

In 1377, Beatrice Scala, Bernadò Visconti's wife, chose it as the capital of the "Wonderful Country". The statutes "Riperiae lacus Gardae" stated that the Podestà Salò had the title of Captain and had jurisdiction over the confederate centres. Beatrice della Scala reinforced the Salodian walls and built a new Castle, of which nothing remains today. Sansovino built the palace of the Captain Rector (now the town-hall), while during the XVth-XVIth cent. the Cathedral, a wonderful example of Gothic-Renaissance style, took its form. There are the two interesting entrance gates of the town (1463); one, the gate of the fortress, faces toward Brescia and the other, St. John's, at the opposite end, within which the older part of the hamlet is enclosed. From the Autumn of 1943 to the Spring of 1945 Salò characterized the last period of fascism, known as the "Republic of Salò". Among the famous men who were born at Salò we must remember Gaspare Bertolotti (1540-1609) known as Gasparo of Salò, a famous maker of string instruments, inventor of the violin, whose bust, by the Salodonian sculptor Angelo Zanelli who also planned the Altar of the Fatherland, is kept in the town-hall.

TO SEE. The Cathedral in Gothic-Renaissance style of the XV-XVIth cent.; the Captain Rector's Palace, a work of Sansovino; the Clock Tower of the XVth cent. In the cluster of houses of Barbarano there is the Terzi-Martinengo Palace of the XVth cent. with a park full of fountains, built by the Marquis Sforza-Pallavicino, Admiral of the Venetian Republic.

The Cathedral. An original inscription dates the laying of the first stone back to the 7th October 1452. The designers—writes Brother Ursula in

SALÒ. Panorama.

SALÒ. Panorama.
SALÒ. The Cathedral of St. Mary the Annunciated (XV cent.).
The first stone was laid in 1453. The façade with a triangular
gable has two Gothic doors with rectangular lights and central door in Renaissance style. ▼

SALÒ. The Cathedral of St. Mary the Annunciated in Venetian-Gothic style. At the far end the fifteenth century altar
piece by Bartolomeo da Isola Dovarese with the wooden
statues by P. Bussola. At the top: the Gothic Crucifix by Giovanni da Ulma. ►

the "Chronacle"—were inspired by the Veronese church of S. Anaestesia. The modifications undergone with time have not changed the unity of the building. There is an excellent equilibrium among the three aisles; with the cylindrical stone columns in relief; the crossed vaults, both of the central aisle and of the lateral ones, are enriched with late-Gothic elements. The works of art are numerous: the gran polyptych—finished in 1476—is by Bartolomeo da Isola Dovarese (the big flowery, Gothic frame) and by the Milanese Pietro Bussolo (among the statues which he signed is that of the Madonna with Child). Also prominent are the statues and the crucifix on the ambones by Giovanni da Ulma (1400); the crib and the adoration of the wise men, by Zenon Veronese and Celesti respectively; the chapel of the Blessed Sacrement is by the Cremonese Malosso (the right hand part is by Bertanza). In the baptistry there are works by Romanino. On the facade, never completed, is the portal, which was carried out from 1506 to 1509 and attributed to Antonio della Porta and to Gasparo da Cairano.

SALÒ. Panorama.

GARDONE RIVIERA

This is one of the most elegant and beautiful areas of the Lake for the variety and magnificence of its vegetation due to the mildness of the climate. It is a famous, international holiday resort lying among delightful hills, large gardens, villas and sumptuous hotels. The inland offers interesting walks with exceptionally beautiful views.

HISTORY. The birth-date of Gardone Riviera is rather recent even if we have some proofs of an ancient past. The small town rose at the end of the last century. Luigi Wimmer, a pioneer of the hotel industry, born in Germany, but who fought for the Italian independence, gave it a particular boost. He arrived at Gardone in 1880, took a liking to the place, characterized by a constant and mild climate even in winter. He built hotels, urged different initiatives, and created contacts with the cosmopolitan world. Year by year the tourist resort of Gardone took shape, with the enchanting promenade, the grond hotels, the Alba villa, the Casino. These buildings of different styles testify to the tastes of the cosmopolitan tourists who enlivened the small town at the beginning of the century. In 1921 the poet Gabriele D'Annunzio came to Gardone Riviera and settled at Cargnacco Villa, transformed into the monumental complex of the Vittoriale.

TO SEE. The Vittoriale of the Italians; Hruska Botanical Garden.

GARDONE RIVIERA. Panorama.

The Vittoriale of the Italians. Accessible from Vittoriale Square, its architectural design, with arches, is very beautiful. In front of the portal the dramatic architecture of the Parish Church stands out. After passing through the portal you reach the "Pilo del Piave" dominated by a statue of Arrigo Minerbi. On the right there is the open air theatre (where every summer ancient and modern plays are performed). Here the landscape of the Isle of Garda with the "Fortress of Manerba"

GARDONE RIVIERA. The complex of buildings and monuments which comprise the "Vittoriale degli Italiani" was carried out at the wish of the poet Gabriele D'Annunzio by the architect G.C. Moroni.

in the background makes a dramatic sight. Advancing through a big arch you reach Esedra, where there is the small temple where Gabriele D'Annunzio was buried till 1963. A narrow staircase leads to the Auditorium where the aeroplane Sva, in which the poet flew over Vienna on 9 August 1918, is kept. On the right of the Auditorium is the d'Annunzio museum (extra ticket needed), prepared in the building called "Schifamondo", where the life and work of Gabriele D'Annunzio is documented by antiques. From the small balcony of the Auditorium you can see the whole of the small Dalmatian square, the heart of the Vittoriale with the Dalmatian pillar placed on two large millstones to press olives. The building of "Schifamondo" towers over the square; eastward there is the Priory, the abode of Gabriele D'Annunzio (closed to the public) where the most authentic relics of the poet's life are kept. Descending the stairs towards the lake you reach, on the right, the grave of Princess Maria D'Annunzio di Montenevoso, the poet's wife. In the portico of the Schifamondo there is the Fiat 4 car, in which D'Annunzio led the march from

The open-air Theatre.

Detail of the prow of the ship "Puglia".

The Dalmatian Square and the façade of the Priory.

STUDY where the writer worked.

FIAT 4 automobile in which Gabriele D'Annunzio led the march from Ronchi to Fiume during the night of 11 to 12 September 1919.

The aeroplane in which D'Annunzio flew over Vienna on 9 August 1918.

Sala del Mappamondo, the Map Room.

Motor torpedo boat which took part in the fighting (10-11 February 1918 "Buccari's jet").

Piave Pilium.

Priory façade.

Prow of the ship Puglia. ▶

Arcade with coat of arms of the Prince of Mount Nevoso. ▶

Chapel of D'Annunzio memories.

Entry to Piave Pilium.

Cast room (Museum).

Lyre room (dining room).

Ercole Sibellato "Blind Seer".

Aviation window (Museum).

Museum entryway (war relics).

Vestibule (or Priory entrance).

Ronchi to Fiume. Turning right from the portico you reach the Aligi alley leading to the "Dolphin's Fountain" into which flows the water of a mountain stream.

On the right, through an arch covered with ornaments is the Mausoleum which keeps ten sepulchres, arranged in a ring, with the mortal remains of the poet's companions in arms; in the central sepulchre, in 1963, they placed D'Annunzio's remains. To the South of the Mausoleum you can see the ship "Puglia" placed on an abutment, in a sea of green. The gardens are very interesting; you can reach them through a portal in the portico of the Priory.

GARDONE RIVIERA. Villa Alba (XIX cent.). The Loggia of the Caryatids. ▶

GARDONE RIVIERA. Villa Alba (XIX cent.). Neoclassical Palladian style.

TOSCOLANO-MADERNO

This is a very important centre formed by two towns, Toscolano and Maderno, blended into a single aggregate stretching on the Gardesana. Toscolano is prevailingly an industrial and a cottage-industry centre, while Maderno, stretching into a picturesque gulf, with a wonderful promenade among villas and gardens is almost exclusively a tourist centre. It is much frequented for the mildness of its climate and its charming position.

HISTORY. According to a legend, the ancient, mysterious town of Benaco, which sunk into the lake owing to an earthquake (about 243 A.D.), was built near Toscolano. We know that near Toscolano there was a Roman oppidum: the remains of a beautiful villa belonging to the Nonii-Arii family have come to light during several excavations. You can find some of the lapidary material of the villa in Verona; other parts have been joined on to the facade of the Church. A memorial tablet on the bell tower, bears a dedication of the Benacesi to Marco Aurelio. Towards the second half of the XIVth century, paper mills, which were valued even in the Far East for their strong paper, were built; while the art of printing flourished in the XVth century. In 1475 Gabriele di Pietro from Treviso, composed a "Donatus pro perulis" in Scalabrino Agnelli's printing-house. Maderno already existed as a town in 969. Barbarossa granted it a conditional independence. It was the chief town of the Riviera of Brescia till 1377 when Beatrice della Scala chose Salò instead, which became the capital of the "Wonderful Fatherland". About 1606 the Gonzaga of Maderno built a holiday villa looking on to the Gulf of Maderno. However the festive residence had only a brief existence. When it was left by the Gonzaga it soon went to ruin and nothing remains of it.

The Church of St. Andrew (XIIth century). It is the Lombardian reduction of St. Zeno the Great, the greatest Romanesque-Veronese monument. The facade mirrors the three aisles inside; the moulding of the door with an arc in the exact centre, closed by a lunette is—writes Gaetano Panazza—"rich and lively, among the most noble of the Romanesque churches". The high and narrow window, still on the facade, recalls the Romanesque windows of Southern Italy.
The inside, with three aisles, has undergone the most changes. Around the XVth century three columns on each side were removed and the monofore windows and doors closed to build altars. The pulpit, placed against the second pillar on the left, is from 1565. In 1580, on the orders of

View from Mount Maderno.

St. Carlo Borromeo, the crypt was destroyed reducing the level of the church to its present state. Particularly curious is that on an upturned block in the left hand corner of the portal, a carved Roman biga can be seen, an obvious sign that in the construction of this church, material from buildings of an earlier era were used. The beautiful belltower dates from 1469.

TO SEE. *The Parish Church of Toscolano:* it keeps 22 large pictures by Andrea Celesti representing stories of the Gospel and of St. Peter. You can admire other paintings by Celesti, of biblical themes, in Delai Palace in the old port; *the Church of St. Andrew*, at *Maderno*, of the XIIth cent, Romanesque style.

MADERNO. General views.

MADERNO. Church of St. Andrew (XII cent.). Detail of the Corinthian style capitals with very old sculptures. An old fresco in the semicircle (Madonna and Child between two Saints).

The Church of St. Andrew (XII cent.). The interior with three aisles, the pillars with a frieze of varied and interesting capitals. Traces of ancient frescoes on the walls.

St. Andrew's Church (XII cent.). The harmonious façade is a masterpiece of Lombard Romanesque architecture.

GARGNANO

A characteristic, picturesque village pleasantly situated among the green of the olive trees and the blue of the sky and the Lake. There are some beautiful walks in its environs; a road with won-

BOGLIACO. Bettoni Villa, main stair-case. Architect A. Marchetti (XVIII cent.).　▶

GARGNANO. The port and lakeside.

derful views leads to Lake Idro, passing through the beautiful hilly zone of Valvestino.

HISTORY. Gargnano is mentioned as early as 973; in fact, it is cited in a rescript for a donation to the cathedral of Verona. In the middle of the XIIIth cent. the Franciscans founded a convent and in 1285 built the Church consecrated to St. Francis. In 1331 John of Bohemia gave it as a fief to the Castelbarco. A century later the village became a part of the "Wonderful Fatherland" and the chief town of a "quadra" i.e. a group of villages. It was a prosperous centre for olive and lemon growing and was embellished, in the XVIIth cent. by the Bettoni Villa, one of the finest of

GARGNANO. The cloister of the convent of the Franciscan Friars (XII cent.).

BOGLIACO. Bettoni Villa. Central Hall. Frescoes by G. Galliari (XVIII cent.).

Garda. During the "Republic of Salò" it gave hospitality to Mussolini and his family in the two Feltrinelli Villas. One of the two Villas, given to the University of Milan, is the site of the Summer courses for foreigners.

TO SEE. *St. Francis of Assisi.* In 1289 the Franciscans built a church of which only the heavily altered exterior remains. The facade which is very similar to that of the church of St. Francis in Brescia, is divided by pillars into three partitions; the elegant stone portal has an arch with a full curve. The inside was redone in the XVIIth and XVIIIth centuries. The quadrangular cloister from the XIIIth century shows Venetian influence, with the rigid arches cast among the circular columns, which are decorated at the base with little protective foils and small capitals decorated with cedar or lemon leaves of oustanding beauty.

The Parish Church of St. Martin. The parish church is situated in the highest part of the village, on top of the little hills. According to the expert Conforti it sits on the site of a more ancient church. The early design of the church probably belonged to a Trentine architect. In 1837 it was decided to trust its completion to Vantini, the celebrated Brescian architect who, "inspired by the majestic, pagan temples, conceived a panthenon with an oval shape". The church holds paintings by Bertanza and by G.B. Casari. On the main altar there is a Madonna attributed to Moretto. Of the early architecture there remains the bell-tower, which is from the Renaissance.

The eighteenth century Bettoni Villa in Bogliaco, belonging to three orders, with abundant baroque grounds, the gran rococo stairways, the nymphs and statues by Domenico Cignaroli. Interesting paintings by Celesti are kept in the hall.

Feltrinelli Villa (where Mussolini stayed for a certain period of time): the *Church of the Crucifix* in Bogliaco.

BOGLIACO. *Bettoni Villa. Italian gardens by the architect V. Pierallini (XVIII cent.).*

GARGNANO. *Feltrinelli Villa. Mussolini's residence during the Republic of Salò.*

TIGNALE (m. 680)

A delightful village with a tourist-agricultural economy sitting on a rocky tableland 600 metres high, and offering beautiful views over the Lake and the surrounding mountains. On a rock, almost perpendicular to the water, there is the

TIGNALE. Sanctuary of the Madonna of Monte Castello. ▶

TIGNALE. Monte Baldo in the background.

Sanctuary of Madonna di Monte Castello, overlooking all the south basin of the Lake. The Municipality, which has its headquarters at Gardola, consists of several villages attractively situated on the green tableland.

HISTORY. The first inhabitants of this area were probably the Cenomani: one of their Gods was Bergimo to whom small temples were erected. Under Tiberius, during the Roman invasion, the hamlet was aggregated to Brescia. In 1212 its economy improved considerably thanks to the Counts of Lodrone, masters of Bagolino, who had numerous estates here. At the end of the XIVth cent., different dominations caused the economic decline of this hamlet with very heavy impositions. In 1385 Tignale passed under the Visconti and in 1404 it became again a fief of the Bishop of Trento and three years later, it became part of the "Serenissima" (Venice). The emperor Maximilian rode through these villages with his army in 1509; in 1700, with the Treaty of Campoformio the Gardola River marked the boundary between the Austro-Hungarian Empire and the Cisalpine Republic.

TO SEE. The Sanctuary of Madonna di Monte Castello, a national monument perched on a rock 77m from the headland. Inside there are frescoes of the school of Giotto and illustrations on copper by Palma the Young.

Sanctuary of Monte Castello. On this delightful hillock, according to popular tradition, was the altar to the pagan God Bergimo of the ancient Cenomani, the first inhabitants of Tignale, later changed into Mary's altar by the patient apostolate of the martyr St. Virgil (380-405 A.D.), the Bishop of Trento. The people of Trento built a fortress, which belonged to them until 1349, on this rocky spur of primary strategic importance, in the year 1000, in front of the little temple.

It underwent many historical events during the centuries; it passed under the Scaligeris rule, under the Duke of Milan Gian Galeazzo Visconti in 1385, under Pandolfo Malatesta and again under the Scaligeri until 1797. The transformation of the Temple Castle was begun by the Bishop of

Brescia, Berardo Maggi, after the battle between the people of Brescia and Trento on the 13th of March 1283.

SANCTUARY OF MONTE CASTELLO. Interior.

XV cent. frescoes.

TIGNALE. Mary at the Temple. Board on copper by Palma.

TREMOSINE

Tremosine sits on a green tableland with rocky walls almost perpendicular to the Lake; from this terrace, which is a continuation of the Tignale tableland, stretching as far as Limone, you can admire outstandingly beautiful views. The town

and its clusters of houses can be reached from the port of Campione through a road winding steeply up the sides of the mountain and entering the spectacular ravine of Brasa.

HISTORY. It was undoubtedly the beauty of the place which drew an Etruscan population here in very ancient times. Its presence is revealed by the famous memorial tablet of Voltino (kept in the museum of Brescia), a real puzzle for paleographers and philologists; the first four lines are in Latin, the last two in Etruscan or in the dialect of a primitive people. There are traces of other periods and of very industrious peoples: the castle (only a few remains) and the church of Pieve (VIth cent.) which has conserved intaglio works.

TREMOSINE. XVIIth century organ.

TREMOSINE. Parish Church. High Altar.

The chest in the Sacristy by G. Lucchini.

The parishchurch of Tremosine is one of the most ancient of West Garda; it is perched on a rocky spur leaning out on the lake. The church, built around the end of the VI century A.D. was rennovated many times; the bell-tower, a square-shaped tower with a conical dome, was added to the temple in the X century A.D. In 1712 the dean Don Rambottini carried out the enlargement of the church with a new span and the sacristy. Inside there are the interesting intaglios of the VII century organ; the choir seats and the table in the sacristy, with very fine baroque style intaglios by Giacomo Lucchini of Condino, are more recent.

Panorama.

LIMONE

Limone is a characteristic, picturesque village behind rocky walls leaning out on the Lake in a pretty inlet among gardens, olive and lemon plantations. Well protected from the winds, it enjoys a very mild climate. Its country cottages, the small, pretty fishing harbour, the narrow roads, give an air of character to this place much frequented by tourists. There are suerb views from the surrounding hills. Limone has recently had a great increase in tourist and hotel facilities and now it is one of the most comfortable places of the lake.

HISTORY. Its name derives perhaps from limen, meaning frontier, or from the cultivation of lemons which once were grown here (as the surviving lemon hauses show). This village is mentioned as early as 1000; in 1200 Brescia had to defend it from the feudal lords of Arco. The small town still keeps that particular charm described by D.H. Lawrence and which conquered Ibsen, too. Daniele Comboni, missionary in Africa and the founder of the Cambonian Order was born in a villa among the olive trees in the locality of Tesol.

TO SEE. The parish church of the XVIIth cent. with the beautiful pictures by Celesti and an artistic wooden crucifix of the XVIIth cent.; S. Rocco Church (XIVth cent.); S. Pietro del Moro Church (XIIIth cent.); St. John's Bridge; Bettoni Palace; Finance Palace.

St. Benedict's church was built in 1685 on the site of a more ancient one (IX-X cent.). From 1693 to 1709 five altars were built inside, four made of valuable marble, one with scagliola, with arabesques of great value. Noteworthy are: Andrea Celesti's pictures (XVIII century), the high altar-piece ascribed to the Veronese school, the statue of the Virgin of Graces (XV cent.), a boxwood crucifix of the XVIII century. In the sacristy, a table, a valuable intaglio work of baroque style by Giacomo Lucchini of Condino (1718) with finely carved drawers and doors.

LIMONE. The port.

St. Benedict's Church. Adoration of the Magi by A. Celesti (XVII cent.).

The port.

A delightful view through the luxuriant vegetation. ►

The Supper of Levi. By A. Celesti (XVIII cent.).

LIMONE. The ancient Church of S. Rocco (XIV cent.). High Altar.

LIMONE. Picturesque houses.

RIVA DEL GARDA

This important, busy tourist centre on the north part of the Lake stretches from the slopes of Mount Rocchetta to Mount Brione, which divides it from Torbole. It enjoys a mild climate which favours a luxuriant vegetation. The promenade along the Lake is among the most beautiful and elegant with many hotel complexes which blend well into the natural surroundings. Many roads depart from Riva, which is an important cross-roads; the most important are: the one to Trento, going through the beautiful valley of the river Sarca, and the one of Tonale that, in the first part, climbs up the rock, into which it is dug perpendicular to the Lake with a succession of splendid and dizzying views, and reaches Lake Ledro, where you can see the remains of a pile-dwelling village of the stone age. At about 3.5 km from Riva is the interesting "Varone Falls" which cascades into a rocky gorge making an attractive natural display.

HISTORY. Riva was certainly inhabited by the Romans as the numerous important archaelogical discoveries prove. The enigmatic epigraph on which someone named Claudia Severa is said to have charged the nautical boarding-school of Riva to put flowers on her husband's grave every year, is well known to scholars. The town, if the memorial tablet is exact, was the seat of a Boarding School of Helmsmen. We know, for certain, that the area was ascribed to the Fabia tribe. The first official document mentioning Riva is of 983 when the Emperor Ottone II committed the town to the care of the Bishops of Verona. In the XIIth cent. the area definitely belonged to the Prince Bishops of Trento. Later it belonged to the Scaligeri, the Visconti of Milan, the Counts of Tirolo and was fiercely contested in the XVth cent. during the Venetian wars. In 1441 by the peace treaty of Cremona, it was given to the Venetians who rebuilt the Fortress, built the present City Hall and the Bastion. The Serenissima government lasted till 1509, when the town was occupied by the troops of P.V. Giorgio III of Naydek. In 1521 it was brought back to the Church of Trento by Bernardo Clesio. In 1703 it was ravaged by the French under General Vendome during the Spanish succession war. In 1796, it was occupied by Napoleon's troops, in 1806 it was aggregated to Bavaria, and in 1810 to the Kingdom of Italy; later it was reoccupied by Austria. After the war of 1915/18 it was annexed to the Kingdom of Italy.

◄ *Panorama.*

◄ *Dock and lakeside.*

◄ *RIVA DEL GARDA. The fort (XII cent.). Seat of the Museum.*

RIVA DEL GARDA. Varone Falls. The water cascades into a narrow chasm from a height of 85 metres.

RIVA DEL GARDA. St. Mark's Gate in the ancient boundary wall.

TO SEE. You can start your visit of the town in the picturesque, 3rd November Square, near the Lake. The Square is embellished with porches of the XIVth cent. built by Guglielmo de Frissoni of Como. Towards the lake you can see the City Hall, once called "Dei Provveditori" and the Pretorio Palace joined on, built by the Scaligeri in 1383. Through the ancient Burned Gate, which opens between the two fine buildings, you can reach S. Rocco Square which still keeps the rustic -lordly aspect of the old Riva. In 3d November Square, eastward, there is the Apponale Tower (the symbol of Riva), 34 m high, built in the XIIth cent. and raised higher in 1555. Beyond the channel surrounding it there is the massive construction of the Fortress of the XIIth cent. with four square angular towers, reduced to the height of the roofs by the Austrians in 1850, except the corbelled Keep, which defends the drawbridge. It was enlarged by the Scaligeri, the Visconti, the Venetians, by Bernardo Clesio and transformed into barracks by the Austrians in the XIXth cent.

From the courtyard full of Roman remains you can go up to the municipal museum (the history of Riva is illustrated on the walls). The fortress houses the Auditorium, where concerts, various exhibitions and congresses are held . Behind the Fortress, in a wonderful position, are the east gate gardens and the beach with olive trees. The baroque Church of the Virgin, the most precious monument of Riva rises northward. It was built in 1611 thanks to Gaudenzio Madruzzo, governor of Riva and Arco. Then there is the baroque church of the Assumption of the Blessed Virgin Mary, St. Joseph's and St. Michael's churches.

The Church of the Virgin. This is perhaps Riva's most precious monument. It was built in 1611, thanks to the impetus of Gaudenzio Mandruzzo, the governor of Riva and Arco. The church has an extremely elegant baroque style, owed, it is assured, to the design of a Portugese architect whose name has unfortunately been lost. The influence of Spanish architecture stands out even in the external structure. On the inside, which is rich and sumptous, the stucco-work of Rieti is very vivid. The crucifix with the Madonna on the first altar on the left is worth noting; on the other three altars, the altar pieces of Palma il Giovane (St. Charles, St. Gerolamo and St. Onofrio). Among the painters who have frescoed this church are Turri d'Arezzo, Bartolomeo Mangiarino da Salò (a presbyterian), Pietro Ricchi called the Lucchese. Kept in the sacresty are very fine intaglio wardrobes and furniture, probably the work of carvers from Trento and Val Gadena.

RIVA DEL GARDA. View of the old Bastion.

RIVA DEL GARDA. The Church of the Virgin.

Inside the dome. Frescoes by Teofilo Turri of Arezzo.

Church of the Virgin. Interior. ▶

Christ on the Cross, by Guido Reni.

TORBOLE-NAGO

The little port. ▶

Views.

Two characteristic hamlets, the first at the mouth of the Sarca, the second on the north slopes of Mount Baldo, form Torbole, a pretty village on the slopes of the rocky hill of Castel Penede, in a

The house where the German poet Goethe stayed.

charming position with a mild climate and a luxuriant vegetation of palms, oleanders, olives and laurels. Goethe stayed at Torbole during his travels in Italy and described the beauty of these places captivated by the wonderful sight of its natural surroundings. The small town, an important and busy place has excellent tourist and hotel facilities. The hamlet of Nago is remembered for the passage of the Venetian ships that were lifted from Mori up Mount Baldo and let down into the Lake at Torbole during a war between the Venetians and the Visconti which broke out in 1437.

HISTORY. The name of Torbole is bound to the famous battle in water of 1439 that resulted in the Venetians taking over the whole area from the Visconti. The undertaking was conceived by Francesco Sforza and led by Stefano Contarini. To transfer six galleys and 25 boats, from the Adige to Garda, by land, they employed two thousand oxen and hundreds of people.

TO SEE. The parish church of Torbole, consecrated to St. Andrew, on a height showing beautiful views. The altar-piece of the main altar, representing St. Andrew's martyrdom, a masterpiece of the painter Cignaroli of Verona (1706-1770) is very valuable. The parish church of Nago with a fine Renaissance portal; a memorial tablet remembers the famous jurist Scipio Sighele. The Longobardian Church of St. Zeno (Nago) on a hill near the Scaligeri tower. The small port of Torbole with the Customs Hall; the remains of Castel Penede; the "Giants' Potholes".

MALCESINE

This picturesque small town is situated on the riviera of the East Gardesana, on the slopes of Mount Baldo, among a luxuriant vegetation of olives, cypresses and oleanders. The superb castle of the Scaligeri of the XIIIth cent. rises on a promontory perpendicular to the Lake. Malcesine is a health-resort and a famous and busy tourist place. Mount Baldo cableway carries you, in a

short time, from the mediterranean climate of the Lake to a height of 1800m showing beautiful panoramas. At the end of the beautiful promenade there is a wonderful bay with the small "Isle of Dreams" one of the most charming places of the Lake.

HISTORY. Its etymology is not simple; perhaps Malcesine derives from Melissineum (bosom of the honey), or Malcesine (a well-established spot). Once it was certainly a fortified place, defended by the fortress. Its population enjoyed au-

MALCESINE. Panorama.

The port.

MALCESINE. The Scaligero Castle (XIII-XIV cent.). ▶

tonomy during several periods: the Bishop of Verona, after 1000, granted it various rights so Pope Eugene III let its inhabitants use coin and measures of their own. But the history of Malcesine is particularly bound to the domination of the Scaligeri. It was in the XIIth cent. that, on a spur perpendicular to the waters, in a panoramic position, they built the powerful Castle the scene of many events, which was later partly destroyed

and then rebuilt as you can see from the different styles of some parts. The domination of the Scaligeri was followed by Austria's for 16 years, by the Visconti's and then the Carrara's. The Republic of Venice gave wide autonomy to the population, confederated with other communes, to form the "Gardesana of the Waters". It was a long, enlightened domination which left deep marks on the village. It lasted 450 years from 1351 to 1797 with the short interruptions of the Visconti and the Maximilians of Austria and the French from 1805 to 1814. After the fall of Venice it was taken by Austria, who transformed it into a fortress and kept it for 51 years until 1866. Many famous people, such as Goethe who, passing through the Alps, started his voyage through Italy from Lake Garda, have stayed Malcesine. On the morning of 13th September 1786, the poet visited Malcesine and the Castle and, struck by

its beauty, drew a sketch on a sheet of paper. The poet drew the attention of people who thought he was a spy and he had difficulty in proving his identity. The poet's stay is now remembered by a bust and several memorial tablets, including one on the wall of the inn of the town, immediately behind the Town Hall, where he stayed.
TO SEE. The Castle of the XIIIth cent., rebuilt many times, is divided into the lower small palace and the upper one and is formed by three courtyards; in the second there is a bust of Goethe. The most ancient part is formed by a stone square-embattled fence; the central one shows swallow-tailed battlements. From the outer yard you can reach the small balcony with a beautiful view of the bay. In the Castle there is a little museum with natural history collections and historical relics. The Captains' Palace, near the port, seat of the Commune in 1500, was the

residence of the Captain of the Lake during the period of the Scaligeri, and of the Venetian Republic. The parish church with a famous "Deposition" by Gerolamo Libri. The Madonna of the Rosary Church with many marble works. The picturesque port of Cassone, a hamlet of Malcesine. Beyond Cassone 200m from the shore there is the islet of Trimellone, where in the Xth cent. a castle was built and then destroyed in 1158 by Barbarossa. Now the islet, once an Italian fort, is a desolate sight owing to the burst of explosions during the last war.

Parish Church. The XVI century parish church stands out among the low topped olive trees. It is particularly richly endowed with works of art and with many precious marbles (note the marble throne of the high altar of 1796, used to display the Holy Sacrament). In front of the tabernacle is the statue with Christ in the tomb between angels and the arch of the patron saints of the Church, Benigno and Caro. The two saints are al-

so portrayed on the altar-piece by Brusasorci. The frescoes representing the Deposition (the work of Girolamo dei Libri) were brought here from the Church of St. Mary of the Organ in Verona. Note the works by the painters Felice Boscaratti (Elijah and Rebecca, Abigail and David), Cialfini (altar-piece of Saints Benigno and Caro), and Odoardo Perini (in the Presbytery).

Church of the Madonna of the Rosary. Built in 1600, it is also known as Madonna of the Fountain, because of the fountain in the square opposite. This Church also has a number of outstanding works in marble (the Eighteenth Century High Altar). Some interesting paintings of the 1600's and 1700's (Madonna and Child and Saints Nicolò da Tolentino and Rocco; the work of Nicolò Crontani).

MALCESINE. Panorama.

THE TOWNS OF MOUNT BALDO

The chain of Mount Baldo (55 km, long, and from 10 to 12 km wide) is among the most important of the Pre-Alps. It is divided into two parts by the Bocca di Navene (1430 m): northward the Trent Baldo culminating in the Altissimo di Nago (2079 m); southward the Verona Baldo culminating in Cima Valdritta (2218 m). The two sides of Verona Baldo look different; the west one is naked, steep, cut by ravines, with a few oases of trees, the east one is more uneven and intersected by longitudinal valleys, with green pastures but no woods.

S. Zeno di Montagna (583 m) is a pretty, small town on the south-west part of Mount Baldo which overlooks almost all the lake of Garda and the mountains behind, as far as the chain of Adamello.

Caprino Veronese (254 m). A picturesque hamlet at the foot of Mount Conca, in a valley rich in olives, vineyards and fruit-trees. At Costermano there is a German war graveyard where the bodies of 22,000 fallen soldiers are buried.

Ferrara di Montebaldo (856 m). A hdiday and a mountain resort, which lies in a valley opening at the foot of Mount Baldo.

BRENZONE

It is an interesting health resort formed by many villages: Castelletto, Assenza; Porto, Pai, Marniga, Magugnano, some of which lie at the foot of Mount Baldo, along the Gardesana road, and others on the slopes among olive yards and gardens.

HISTORY. The Roman town of Brunzonium conserves many traces of past events. In the XIIth cent. at Castelletto a convent was built, now consigned to the Nuns of the Holy Family; while Assenza, the ancient town of Menarolo (so called because food-stuffs and fodders were carried to the landing-stage) boasts a church of the XIVth cent.

TO SEE. The Convent of the Nuns of the Holy Family (at Castelletto) of the XIIth century with interesting frescoes of the XIVth cent. The small church of St. Zeno (1 km from Castelletto) of the XIIth cent. in a small churchyard full of cypresses, with an asymmetrical facade and internal frescoes of the XVth cent. The remains of the Scaligeri Castle (at Biaza).

CASTELLETTO DI BRENZONE. St. Zeno's Church (XII cent.).
BRENZONE. View. ▶

TORRI DEL BENACO

This is one of the most picturesque villages of the Olive Riviera, placed at the foot of Mount Baldo, in a beautiful area among pines, olive and citron groves. It is joined to Maderno, on the west

of which is Roman, with other interesting remains. The philosopher and mathematican Domizio Calderini, who died in Rome in 1487, was born here. He is remembered in a marble stele

bank of the Lake, by a ferry-boat service for passengers and cars.

HISTORY. According to tradition the Romans called it "Castrium Turrium" because of its numerous towers. It had great importance in the Middle Ages, in fact it was the chief town of the "Gardesana of the Lake" and the seat of the General Council, before this Council passed to Garda. "The Captain of the Lake" gathered the General Council, formed by the 18 confederated towns, to decide the management of the incomes, the defence of rights, the abolition of abuses. You can see some remains of the Roman "castra" in the square of the church where Berengario dated six royal diplomas from Torri in 1009.

In 1383 Antonio della Scala rebuilt the manor -house of which three towers have survived, one

near the small church of the Holy Trinity, with an inscription by Poliziano. Among the famous men who stayed in Torri, we remember Andrè Gide who spent, as he wrote in his diary, "wonderful days" here from June to September, in 1948.

TO SEE. The small church of the Holy Trinity, in Calderini Square, with frescoes of the school of Giotto; the XVIIIth cent. facade, of Eccheli Palace with "the small house of the XVth cent." nearby; Berengario's Tower, in Church Square, well preserved remains of the Roman "Castrum Turrium" and the Roman quarter ("el trincerone") of authentic Roman origin; the Cathedral, known for the variety of the marbles used in the altars.

TORRI DEL BENACO. Views.

ST. VIGILIO'S POINT

The promontory of St. Vigilio's Point stretches out into the bright blue of the Lake forming two delightful inlets: one, known as the "Bay of the Sirens" with a small beach, the other forms a small pretty harbour. On the cape of the promontory, among olive groves and cypresses, is the ancient small church of St. Vigilio and the beautiful Guarienti Villa erected in the 16th century and designed by Sanmicheli, with a wonderful park adorned with statues.

GARDA. St. Vigilio's Point and the old church.

GARDA

It lies in the middle of a wonderful gulf with widely curved banks and is protected, nothward, by the slopes of Mount Baldo, southward by the Fortress, and eastward by low, moraine hills. The Gardesana route, through villas and olive yards unites the town to St. Vigilio's Point, one of the most romantic and famous places of the Lake, much frequented by Italian and foreign tourists at all times of the year. A carriageable, asphalted road leads from Garda to "Spiazzi di Monte Baldo" and the famous Madonna della Corona Sanctuary.

HISTORY. Some traces of settlements from the neolithic period have found on the fortress. Rock inscriptions found in St. Vigilio's Point are also testimony of the ancient inhabitants of these areas. Pagus Romano became important in the Middle Ages because of its Castle, after Charlemagne made it on earldom in 768. From that time Garda gave its name to the Lake, once called Benaco. According to a legend the nuptials of the first of the barbarian queens of Carducci, Teodolinda, were celebrated here. In 950 Queen Adelaide di Borgogna, another barbarian, Carducci queen, Lotario's widow, was held prisoner in the Fortress by Berengario II; she succeded in escaping thanks to the help of a fisherman or a friar, according to the legend, and took refuge at Canossa, marrying Ottone I from Germany, who exiled Berengario, on Christmas evening in 951. There is also the story of Turisendo, a feudal Lord of Gardesana who held out to Barbarossa's siege (1162-63) from the Fortress. This memorable resistence is remembered also by Muratori: "No town in Italy resisted the terrible Augustus, except the Fortress of Garda". The vicissitudes of the Fortress are bound to those of Ottone of Wittesbach, the founder of the House of Bavaria and to the Bishop Alberto of Trento, till 1209 when Ottone IV, after taking it to the Commune, destroyed it. The rule of the Venetian Republic also left important traces. In 1452 the "Antichi Originari" Corporation bought the fishing rights for 3075 gold ducats; to pay that amount the women had to sell their jewels. The history and legends of Garda have been summarised by the poet Carducci in famous lines.

TO SEE. The ancient hamlet with its characteristic lanes; two gates of the medieval town wall are still well-preserved (inside the west gate there is an elegant mullioned window with two

lights). The Gothic-Venetian palace of the Captain of the Serenissima on the small square looking over the lake. The Rennaissance style Fregoso Palace where Bandello stayed; the story of Juliet and Romeo many have been born here. Along the Lake there is Sanmicheli's loggia of the XVIth cent. with a low tower. On the Gardesana road there is the interesting Villa Albertini, shaped like a castle, surrounded by a large park where,on 10 June 1848, King Carlo Alberto received the delegation bringing him the annexation act of Lombardy to Piedmont. Other interesting buildings are: Palazzo Carlotti XVIth century, Palazzetto del Ponte (XVIIIth century), Villa Canossa, Villa Guarienti (at St. Vigilio). The parish church keeps some paintings of Palma il Giovane and Francesco Paglia.

Villa Guarienti, built in the XVIth century by Sanmicheli for the Veronese writer Agostino Brenzone (not open to visitors). The small, ancient Church of St. Vigilio also belongs to the villa. Surrounded by cypresses, with its little bell-tower reflected in the lake, it is an inexhaustible source of inspiration for painters. At the tiny, characteristic port with an inn nearby, it is possible to hire a boat from which to admire the famous view of the little church, from the lake. Beyond the Punta (Point) occupied by the magnificent park of Villa Guarienti, the idyllic Bay of the Sirens, with its limpid waters between olive and cypress trees, is particularly inviting for a bathe. The painter Pisanello (1379-1455) was born in St. Vigilio.

GARDA. Villa Albertini.

The wide bay and the long beach facing a magnificent blue lake. ▶

COSTERMANO

This pleasant agricultural village just inland in the gardesian area is beautifully situated, it is particularly well known to German tourists because on this land the Military cemetery for German soldiers is situated.

The German military cemetery. On the 6th of May 1967, with a sombre but important ceremony, the Cemetery for German soldiers was consecrated. Thus the agreement between the German Federal Republic and the Italian Republic to give dignified burial to the around twenty two thousand corpses of soldiers killed in action in different parts of Northern Italy during the last war, was carried out. Costermano was chosen not just for the evocativeness of the environment, but also for its extremely easy access for the waves of German tourists, who in Garda have always had a reference point for excursions and holidays.

The monumental complex was built on the Guardian heights, in a sheltered valley between the Caprino plain and the gulf of Garda. It took eight years to complete it; the transfering and burial of the corpses was taken care of by the special service of the National German League for the care of War Cemeteries, to whom the Federal Government had assigned the task of achieving the monument.

In fifteen plots 21,920 German soldiers are laid,

previously they were buried in various places in Northern Italy. The cemetery looks like a garden: past the square, in the floor of which a dove, the symbol of peace, stands out, and through the gate, the visitor is struck by the evocative sight of ornamental heather; the roadways contrast with the areas of grass, an emerald carpet, and with the wild woods which have grown up here and there, on the land. The springtime, with the flowering of the roses and various plants, bestows a melting beauty on the environment. A steel cross, eight metres high, visible even from afar, is the highest point, a call to mediation and prayer. Near to the cross there is an altar for the rites.

The tombstones are of brown porphyr; on every grave a tablet lists the names and particulars of the two corpses inside. Small, black crosses complete the complex, also endowed with other buildings like the sacristy and the rooms for the custodians.

The monument is the destination of thousands and thousands of people who many years after the wartime tragedy still carry in their hearts the

living memory of their loved ones. For all of them the monument is a place of reflection, a grim warning to follow the path of peace.

Camandolesi's hermitage is of very ancient origin, but its present structure dates back to 1673. Among the abbots who built it, we have Pietro Ottoboni, who later became Pope Alexander VII and the sixteenth century Latin poet Marcantonio Flamini. The Marchess Alexandra Carlotti Rudini nurtured her calling for religious seclusion here and she retired afterwards into the Carmelo di Monmartre. Her story was described by Prario in his book "Three white dresses for Alexandra". The monastery, abolished in 1810, was returned to the monks in 1885.

BARDOLINO

Bardolino lies in a wonderful position at the foot of hills covered with orchards, olive yards and vineyards producing famous wines. Its open position, its very mild climate, the wide beaches and its environs draw tourists and holiday-makers.

HISTORY. According to some linguists, its name derives from the German, Bardali or Pardali, the name of King Argonauta Auleto's daughter. But even before it had a name, Bardolino was inhabited by populations who already knew the famous wine celebrated during the Roman period; the prehistoric remains, found here, prove it. It was famous for its wine, which was celebrated by Cato and Cassiodoro and reached the tables of Caesar and Catullus who lived between Verona and Sirmione and must have known the area well. The streets of Bardolino still show the Roman mark as does its toponymy which keeps Latin words; certain distances, between two houses, are still called "intercapedines". The name of Bardolino appears for the first time in 807 in a document signed by King Pipino, Charlemagne's son, in his residence in Verona.

During the Middle Ages it was a free Commune, then it passed under the Scaligeri and then to Venice. The passage of the Lansqueenets (1526) who spread grief and ruin is remembered by documents. Under the rule of Venice, Bardolino experienced a benificial development of agriculture and particularly viticulture. Among its famous personalities are the three Betteloni poets, Cesare (1808-58), Vittorio (1840-1910) and Gianfranco (1876-1948), father, son and nephew. The short poem "The Lake of Garda" by Cesare Betteloni, a commendation of the great lake and its people is very well-known.

TO SEE. S. Severo Roman church in Romanesque style with a Longobard crypt (VIIIth cent.) and internal frescoes of the XIIth cent.; S. Zeno Longobard church of the VIIIth cent.

Church of San Severo (XI-XII cent.). An old Romanesque construction of the XI century, it was part of the very ancient Pieve di Garda mentioned in the Diploma of Berengaria in 983 A.D. Restored in the XII century, in the XVth it became a parish church. Then it was neglected and lost its importance during the following centuries. The church has three unequal apses and a number of embrasure windows at the sides. In the interior interesting frescoes represent the visions of the Apocalypse and figures of Apostles and Saints, paintings going back to the XIII century.

CISANO DI BARDOLINO

Church of St. Mary (XI-XII cent.). The first church was built in about 915 on the ruins of a pagan temple; it was rebuilt in the XII century after the earthquake of 1117. An interesting Romanesque style prothyrum or hanging porch protrudes

above the door in the façade. A fresco of a Madonna and Child painted in the niche is from the XVIth century. Some VIII century sculptures decorate the side of the prothyrum: an eagle, a fish, a horse and a horseman. Above, a mullioned window decorated with friezes and dentils and three finely worked stones. The apse is an important work and a true jewel of Romanesque art.

LAZISE

Lazise is a picturesque hamlet still surrounded by the ancient walls with embattled towers, built by the Scaligeri. Lazise, which keeps so many memories of its medieval past, is now the goal of numerous tourists drawn by the distinctive village, which, because of its wonderful position is one of the most beautiful and interesting places of the lake.

HISTORY. Lazise, Lasitium for the Romans, has a very eventful history. The "Corporation of the Natives" the prevailing class of the village, built St. Nicholas' small church in a fine, Romanesque style in about the XIIth century. In the XIth cent., they built the Castle, one of the most interesting of Lake Garda, where the sovereigns of the Holy Roman Empire stayed. It was enlarged by the Scaligeri and the Venetians. Later it was reduced to a ruin. In the XIXth cent., it was restored by Count Buri and now belongs to the family of the Borini Counts. It was very important under the rule of the Serenissima, for Venice had an important shipyard here, interred with the ancient port.

TO SEE. St. Nicholas' Romanesque church, with a very distinctive façade, regular below and formed by broken pieces of earthenware above. Inside it keeps frescoes in Pisanello's style. The ancient Customs Hall beside the Port, built in Venetian style trusses; the Romanesque Tower in the churchyard; if you want, you can visit the Scaligeri's Castle with the keeper's permission. The Castle, the Towers and the embattled walls which surrounded the old Village. The external walls were protected by a deep moat. There were three entrance gates to the Castle: one on the east, the San Zeno Gate (with a mosaic of the Saint); one on the north, the Cansignorio Gate (1375-1376); one on the south, the Gate of the Lion of St. Mark (1405-1797).

The first gate was used by the inhabitants and goods waggons, the other two by the garrison.

LAZISE. The wet dock.

The wet dock and the Church of St. Nicholas.

PESCHIERA DEL GARDA. The Sanctuary of the Madonna del Frassino (Madonna of the Ash Tree), (XVI cent.).

The sanctuary of the Madonna of Frassino. A few kilometres from Peschiera, in a lovely inland position, beside the "serenissima" motorway, stands the sanctuary of the Madonna of Frassino. Here on the 11th May 1510, in extremely sad times of war between Venetians, Spanish, French and Germans, the miraculous event witnessed by a peasant, Bartolomeo Broglia, occurred.

Broglia was working in a vineyard in the Pigna quarter, when, writes the historian Antonio Fappani, he was terrified by the sight of a non-poisonous snake. He immediately thought of a prayer to the Madonna and suddenly right in front of his eyes, among the leaves of an ash tree, a statue of the Virgin appeared, surrounded by light. Ecstatically he fell to his knees giving thanks, and after having kissed the statue he took it home, shutting it in a box.

When he went to take it out he found it was gone. The statue had miracolously returned to the ash tree of the miracle. The good Broglio, considering himself unworthy, recounted the story to the archpriest of Peschiera, don Antonio Cornacchi, who went with the authorities to the place of the apparition. With a solemn procession the statue was transported to Peschiera to the church of the Discipline. But even from there it dissappeared to return to the ash tree of the miracle. It was decided to build a sanctuary on the spot. Work began on the 10th September 1511 and as soon as the temple was finished it was entrusted to the Serviti, passing, a few years later, to the Minori monks. The monument, restored in 1931 to it's early franciscan beauty, holds numerous works of art: a table by Zeno da Verona (1541), a nativity by Paolo Farinati (1560), other works by Farinati and by Astolfi. The 18th century medallions among the arches of the side chapels and the painting above the central door are by Giovanni Simbenati.

The heart of the sanctuary is represented by the chapel where the miraculous statue is kept. The altar-piece is still Farinati's (1560) while of the twelve paintings of the vault and the walls, eleven are by Bertanza da Salò (XVIIIth century) and the twelfth, depicting the blessed Duns Scoto, is by Zambrognini. The two bronze statues are by Prof. R. Banterle.

PESCHIERA DEL GARDA

It is an important tourist and commercial centre on the south-east end of the Lake where the river Mincio flows down. The fortress with the strong ramparts, the high walls and deep ditches surrounding it gives the fine, small town an imposing, austere look.

HISTORY. The history of Peschiera, as the remains discovered during the excavations begun

in the XIXth cent. prove, goes back to prehistoric times. It already existed with the name of "Aritica" in the Roman period and was the seat of a seamans' school. Some historical testimonies remember the stay of Caius Marius, who settled in the fortress when he had to fight against the Cimbri (101 B.C.). It was always a contended centre owing to the strategic importance of its port; in 849 the navy of Peschiera was destroyed by the inhabitants of Verona and the Venetians. It belonged to the Scaligeri (1409), the Gonzaga (1441), Venice (1584-1659). In 1530 Charles V, returning from his coronation in Bologna, stayed in

Peschiera from 20 to 21 April, receiving the Venetians' homage. The town was enlarged and fortified under the Serenissima, according to the plans of Guidobaldo della Rovere and Sanmicheli. In June 1796 Napoleon established his headquarters here. After Campoformio, the fortress belonged to Austria. Alexander I from Russia, the Grand Duke of Tuscany, the King of Naples stayed here, during the Congress of Vienna. It was fortified after the armistice of Villafranca and remained under Austria until 1866 and became one of the fourth fortified towns of the famous Quadrilateral with Verona, Mantova and Legna-

go. In the fortress of Peschiera, King Victor Emmanuel III decided to resist, to the last, on the line of Piave on 8 November 1917.

TO SEE. The double town wall (2250 metres long) and the remains of the fortress. The historical small palace, a work of Sanmicheli, with the famous Congress Hall, keeps antiques of the Renaissance and the war of 1915-18. On the facade there is a memorial tablet of P. Canova, remembering the meeting of the allies on 8 November 1917.

Typical lake fishing.

GARDALAND

Gardaland, created in 1975, is the largest amusement park in Italy and one of the largest in Europe. It is situated on Lake Garda and covers an area of about 400,000 m², half of which is open parkland. Gardaland offers you a unique way to spend a fun-filled day immersed in marvellous natural scenery.

It is the natural surroundings, the greenery and the flowers which give the most pleasurable surprise to the visitor's eye. There are 280,000 seasonal plants, a natural brook - the Dugale - running through the park and broad garden areas, all of which make Gardaland not only an amusement park but a genuine botanical garden.

And added to this is the fun side of Gardaland. The multiple attractions range from a variety of themes and environments, the most famous of which are: the magnificent "Valley of the Kings", an impressive reconstruction of the Egyptian temple of Abu-Simbel; the traditional "Horse Carousel", a faithful reconstruction of an 18th century merry-go-round on two levels; the charming "Colorado Boat", an exciting water ride on tree-trunks through rapids; the "African Safari", a canoe trip through the jungle to discover its inhabitants; and Magic Mountain, sensational thrills in the sky 30 metres up.

In the 1992 season Gardaland will add to its treasures with a spectacular new attraction called "The Privateers" - an exciting adventure aboard a galleon, sailing in swirling seas in the midst of a real battle, attacked by sea creatures which suddenly emerge and accompanied on the voyage by the friendly ghost, the Black Privateer

Throughout the day over 40 shows take place in special areas within the park. There is a theatre with shows by genuine artists, an open-air arena with trained parrots, the Arab market-place with displays of strength and balancing acts and the pavilion where dolphins joke and play with the public.

In addition to all this guaranteed fun, in the midst of green and natural surroundings is a complete services complex with bars, pizza portours, self-service and waiter-service restaurants and a covered picnic area. There is no lack of attractive and colourful shops selling all you could wish for - toys, souvenirs, clothes and jewellery - and all in a happy and relaxed atmosphere.

INDEX OF LOCALITIES